1. CTR+ALT+Del
2. Hamsterdance
3. Brain dump
4. Joey's rainy day
5. Turn out the blank light
6. Cold
7. Dark clouds
8. Superstition
9. Shaved head
10. Not working
11. The phone
12. Vibrate
13. The departed pen
14. Divine operation
15. Madness
16. Vampires: uninduction
17. Addiction 2: War of reality
18. My first love
19. Underworld gods-Traditions and bondage
20. Underworld gods 2- Dreamcatcher
21. The role players
22. Coliseum
23. Don Quixote
24. Battle most fierce
25. Heads or tails
26. Ode to a co-worker
27. Where did we learn to speak
28. The façade of the day
29. The day I almost died
30. Visitor
31. Oh Jonah
32. Hood and cloak
33. Melkor's Boast
34. Kill the dragon
35. Dr. Red eye
36. Heartbreaker
37. February 14
38. Busted
39. Scars
40. What do you do when God is calling?

CTR+ALT+DEL

My system crashes the 11th time!
Red circles surround my eyes
The machine is not responding
Blood pressure reaching new highs
CTR+ALT+DEL

I haven't saved my work in a while
I'm almost done now it's time
And soon I can smile
My thesis on inner city crime
CTR+ALT+DEL

With a yell that fills my dorm
I grab that angering form
I lift it high to destroy, yet don't
I sigh at the passing of a storm
CTR+ALT+DEL

Hamsterdance
There is a hamster in a cage
It's driving all to the newest rage
It bites the bars late at night
This starts the Hamster dance

This disco sounds sort of cool
Till it keeps you up like a fool
The band looks harmless and cute
Don't let fuzzball fool you he's a toot

It spills its food over the side,
Making sounds you can't abide,
It runs in its wheel all the night
It likes it when I turn out the light

Jump up and down and bang your fist
and this is just the start of the list
 Yell and scream shout and hiss
Do the hamsterdance

Waking up at 12 O 'clock
You hear this pet biting, it's time to rock,
Bang your head and pull your hair
Try to kill him with your chair

Are you tired and worn out-
Lower your voice, please don't shout
A few more hours and the sun is up
You put it out you've had enough

You must sleep- your worn out
You rest your head and start at snore
I hate to bother you any more,
But it's time for the hamsterdance

Joey's Rainy Day

"Its raining Joey your getting wet,"
"Oh but mom I can't come in yet"

"Come in right now or you'll catch a cold"
"Oh what superstitions these gron-ups hold"

"If You're out another minute your grounded"
"Such fears ,mom, are quite ill founded"

"Its quit raining and the sun is bright"
"Darn it once again my mom was right"

"I have found adults sometimes tell us true"
"blasted I' m sick in bed achoo."

Turn out the blank light
Well I had just seen a cool show
Talking in words I didn't know
So I wasn't at all prepared
When I emulated, how people stared

All I had said was turn out the light
to speak was within my right
My brother told me not to repeat
"but this word was really neat

Not taking a hint I dropped it again
I paid the price for my careless sin
No more TV for a whole year
Lest I hear a word, causing all to fear

Brain dump
Don't check your brains
So you have heard
But your mind will expand
With the power of the Word

It will be the best trip
You've ever taken
There are no nightmares
When of Christ your partaking

Indeed your intellect will double
Your understanding expand
You will be freed from domination
And the fleshes command

See the foolishness of apes
With the creation of a man
You will dismiss the didactic
Only then will you understand

Cold
Alone in the corner
In a tiny loft
A white mouse shivers
It can not stop

The hungry cat hunts
With predatory skill
The poor little mouse:
It is shivering still

The snow capped yard
Show winters great hold
O poor little mouse:
It shivers with cold

Dark clouds
Up from the graves of ancient past
The pagan gods in Western stance
Riding forth to their final bout
Out from the gates of Olympian's mount

People look back to agricultural days
Norse legends again garner praise
These stone giants again come forth
A tidal wave out of the North

Now digitized consuming culture
Gaze with lust like carrion vultures
Jupiter, Thor, Loci, and Osiris
They have come back through the iris

They dare to challenge the Lord of host
The God of heaven: the Holy Ghost
Christ awaits the lamb and lion
Who are these that dare defy Him

Superstition
Knock-Knock on wood
I don't think you understood
What is an ancient curse?
The recitation of that verse.

Demons prey on such thought,
But what is real and what is not?
If it breeds irrational fear-
There is something full of rot

Under ladders then mistletoe
Some traditions should they go?
Where is my black cat-
You are leaving-why is that?

Shaved head
I've had only one style-
Since I was young.
Guys wear short hair -
That's just how it's done.

Only twice in my life

Have I broken this rule
Once was for money
And the other-
For a girl that I knew

Kept on in basic degree

Myself and my comrades
Of hair we are free
With clippers and razors
Our logic you see

Not working
The computer is down.
I'm twiddling my thumbs-
This not working work
It is far from fun.

My meetings and schedule
All have to wait.
My computer won't work
It won't cooperate

My mind is in neutral
If it is still there
My computer is blank
And I'm pulling my hair!

The Phone
My phone is ringing off the hook
Sales people telling me to read their book
It's a sale barrage like you've never seen
I'm going crazy, just about to scream

Time for work, I get on the phone
I sell this book right from my home
A book how to keep salespeople away
I have a clear conscience its a wonderful day

Vibrate
Hey now, you know the dance
Beginning as the dog starts to prance
Jump all around the room
Chase your dog with a broom
Crawl around on the floor
Toss his bone out the door
Vibrate

Stepping back he starts to whine
Don't worry you're doing fine
Rush out pick him up
Twirl around the confused pup
Begin to shake Elvis style
Or holler some music like Gomer Pyle
Vibrate

Your warmed up, chase him around
 Up the neighborhood by a barking sound
When at last you've lost the game
Sit down and pet the flame
Tired now You both rest
Having once again completed the test
Vibrate

The departed Pen
Listen my friends
Ye erratic persons of skill
Talent is a gift-
Not to be handled as shill
Like a pen departed

Listen to this tale of woe
Of one who went dry
One who grew old
His heart was to die
The day the pen departed

Laureate of inspirational flow;
His heart moved his hand.
His intellect glowed.
Till he was unmanned,
The pen departed

O poor poet he was confused;
How had it withdrawn?
How did he lose-
Now it was gone
That pen departed

Though he sat at his table
Yearning for thought
All he heard was silence;
Where had his love been lost?
The departed pen

Madness
I can see it spreading
That intoxicating disease
That fantasy reality-
Bringing wisemen to their knees

They have been vaccinated
Against the only cure
The power of this germ
In the heat it burns

Like the pressure plate
The all consuming thought
Break off this engagement
Before you are rot

Divine operation
Well old Adam had edgy nerves
The Great physician got a little perturbed
He ribbed Adam but got no change
So he operated on that disjointed knave

Adam woke with a big surprise
There sat Eve by his side
With a coy smile on her mouth
And that is how man found out

Never put God to such a test
Sometimes it's better to let it rest
God's humor and man's mistake
Beauty came- God said awake

Vampires: uninduction
It's a vampire tune; a Gothic twist
A dark story, a deadly kiss.
A move of passion and unbridled lust
There is just one problem-
It is a total bust

Leaving vacant-filling with void
Stealing promise, destroying joy
There is hope of its destruction-
A way to save from soul seduction-
It's the Word-God's instruction.

Addiction 2: War of reality
It's a craving that makes you kneel
It's a feeling that makes life unreal
But it's a lie a fabrication-
Death is its only destination

There's only one way to beat this wolf;
No garlic or superstitious proof
It takes submission to Jesus life
The only joy that makes things right.

Butterflies and dragon snakes-
What is it that makes you wake?
Just when you think you've kicked it
But there's only one way to fix it

You can't be a fake cause it knows
Religion that's okay with this foe
Even sorrow and regret
Cloak this creature of the set

My first Love
Long before girls could enter my mind
I fell in love for the very first time
I fell on my knees; giving You my heart
I was ecstatic I had a brand new start

Your Holy Spirit filled me with a fire
Only asking to be my heart's desire
Gone were my nights of being alone
I had placed you upon the throne

Filling me with joy like the surging ocean
Oh my love what a commotion,
 You caught me, I fell for your advance
Against agape I hadn't a chance

Underworld gods-Traditions and bondage
In certain nations demons are gods
From deals with devils and ancient laws
Shiva's arms seek to push Christ away
Across the Water the emperors betrayed

In scattered huts where smoke filled minds
Medicine calls forth creatures assigned
Chemosh he walks in many guises
The signs of Zodiac fill numerous skies

Communist kingpins worship the state
An unforgiving god in the east he awaits
Inside the beltway and inside of cults
They seek to blind open minded adults

Underworld gods 2- Dreamcatcher
Native Americans called him blessing;
Medicine men drank deep confessing
This net took souls down to death,
That demon brother of said Molech

In the chords of his dark embrace
He fans the temptress gaudy face.
Stealing dreams and numbing minds-
He was born of Nephilim kind.

Yet yea like his fellow beasts:
His time is short to play his peace.
This lord of hell dreams of the pit
In the dungeons of his wit

For long ago he wove his last.
Jesus Christ broke his badge.
Now in fear and hatred's slave:
He weaves his webs of charades.

The Role players
Three players sat at old oak table
To beat the fourth they were unable
Casting spells and using magic arts
This role playing game had captured their hearts

One of them at last summoned his greatest spirit
When all at once they could hear it.
They could smell sulfur and see fiery smoke
The table in front cracked and broke

Darkest night enveloped the room
They felt their spines tingle in fear of doom
A voice of power came from the game
" What is it? You called my name."

When suddenly the 4rth player awoke to truth
 Remembering the faith of his early youth,
He called for help from the one who saves
"Lest we become this creatures slaves"

The presence of God could be felt
Even the demon bowed and knelt
Light shot through the window's glass
The power of God made the spirit pass

God's voice said "take warning and heed
You almost lost your soul from this deed "
Now tell these others how to be free,
Then come all follow me."

Coliseum
Augustine spoke of it with anger:
That dreadful beautiful call
That demon god Coliseum
The crowds thunderous applause

A friend dragged to this vortex
Of this powerful demon's hall
Where the gore and flesh
Keep great crows enthralled

Closing his eyes tight shut
It was to no avail
The roar of the mob
Hit a will so humanly frail

The blood of that drawing
That esoteric temple of doom
Breaks down the family
While empires are consumed

Yet your doom is as the martyrs
An end to your revelry and feats
Your halls shall eventually crumble
Then fallen shall be the great beast

Don Quixote
Roll over quixotic
Your odyssey is noble
But your brain
It is in trouble

Your Spartan routine
Your gallant joust
A laughing stock
Has become your house

The windmill won
Your martial acts
fighting lions
Your brain has cracks

So return
rest your feet
End this sojourn
By the fire's heat

Battle most fierce
Born in a day of demon brood
Possessing her- She was subdued
On the stage the tigress beguiled
Such is the offshoot of destinies child

Only one can free from this cry
Only one can destroy the lie
Only one can cast out the beast
And bring a poor soul to inner peace

On the prowl she manifests
Her flame destroying all regrets
Cast out this unholy ghost
By the love of the Lord of hosts

Heads or Tails?
The dream ends
An alarm sounds
The sweat drips
And the heart pounds

The quarter spins
And flies on high
Two face grins
Will you live or die

But it's not chance
That roils the mind
Or brings oppression
That makes one blind

The hand it reaches
A light turns on
The coin has landed
Right or wrong

Ode to a coworker
He had not a chair but sat on a ball
Was into insanity and total recall
Liked Justin's music –that strange child
An army of one in complete denial

 Never silent-Completely expressive
Over the line and sometimes suggestive
He liked to drive being completely aggressive
In trouble or trim- you could count on the festive

Where did we learn that Lingo
Well I was in my spot on boards when a girl came in and said
"I want one of those like number five things."

Where did we learn to speak
We're not blond, I don't think
Like I'm wondering
Were did we learn to speak
from LA to Chicago, from
New York to Washington
Were did we learn to speak
Sounds kind of strange

Were did we learn to speak
Like totally awesome
Feel like a total geek
Where did we learn to speak
speak with like whatever
dive down learn the lingo
Maybe its cause I'm gringo?
Where did we learn to speak

The façade of the day
It is Five O Clock
The desks are all empty
The building is busy
Workers are leaving
Dropping the façade of the day

Driving away in various array
Both poor and rich
Stripped to the soul
Barren and cold
Shedding all cover
The Facades of the day

So strip this pretense
And all other offense
Let minds cease to gaze
It is all over
And it has been exposed
The façade of the day

The day I almost died
The sky was red and overcast
The warning heat beat down
I was in a fix
Like Tonto gone to town

Whiskey in my saddle
A simple carefree ride
That's how I met my wife
The day I almost died

Hanging on a rope
I knew that I was framed
My wonderful timing
A scapegoat to be blamed
Hanging by this rope
Low on oxygen
When I croaked the word
The preacher said amen

Whiskey in my saddle
A simple carefree ride
That's how I met my wife
The day I almost died

This dangling I'll remember
Till my last day
My limited options-
The judges one horse shae.
For I married his daughter
A sure and honest cure
For behind the iron curtain
They knew I'd behave for sure

Whiskey in my saddle
A simple carefree ride
That's how I met my wife
The day I almost died

Visitor
Halls of darkness trembled
When the lock it broke
Baal that Jezebel worshiped-
From a nightmare woke.

There on his doorstep
Stood the king of grace
Radiant and shining
There to take his place

He seized the keys to death
And locked the devil in
Now men who wish to leave
Can be born again

OH Jonah
In the belly of a whale, in the belly of a fish
Come on mates, Lets serve up a dish
A delicious dish, A fantastic tale
 Of Jonah

God told him to go, and spread His word
To Go to a people who had never heard
But He didn't like these people around
So he got on a ship and sailed out of town
He sailed on a ship, he sailed far away
But no matter how he tried, he couldn't get away
So God put him in confinement for 3 whole days
Poor Jonah

Well he went on God's mission, he told how it was
then he complained, God is too merciful to us
Then God came and showed him the truth
Of Jonah

Hood and cloak
The figure turned
With eyes that burned
That penetrated my very soul

Those dark cold rings
That steel that clings
A dagger pierced my heart

The tears that dropped
Betrayal stopped
Ensnared in mail twine

Now look in my eyes
And surmise
The veil has been torn away

Melkor's boast
(Based on the world of Tolkien)
I was chained in darkness
My own mind' assignation
But I see a crack in it
To bring desolation

I will reclaim my greatness
Create my own song
I will ascend among children
For the elder are gone

I will repaint the picture
And claim my old power
The earth will turn bright
And heaven be devoured

Kill the Dragon
(Based on the oath by Frank Peretti)
Out of the darkness I feel a cold stare.
The dragon is waiting, I know he's out there.
The hairs on my head are all standing on end.
The mark on my heart
Makes it impossible to pretend.

I can't kill the dragon till it's been removed.
This part of my heart this lovely dark root.
"I have you now and I'll never let you go"
These words in my dreams
Of my passionate throw

The cold chilling voice: the numbing affect,
If I cease to careI 'll become dragon breath.
So I must repent and kill the serpent inside
Before I hunt this dangerous worm
On his own mountainside

Dr Red Eye
Hear now this short rendition ,
Of one astute well known physician,
The great tragedy and great loss
The fate of the mysterious practician
A missionary and medical man
He fell into darkness and submission
His own terrible glass eyed prescription

The Dark Continent took his core
When he tried to learn its lore
Though he saved many lives
He lost his soul in his pride
When he lost part of his sight
He met a shaman and changed sides
O the sad tale of Dr. Red eye

Now his patients were the elite
His fame spread to every street
Babylon's power grew again
He owned the minds of many men
But his schemes his switched allegiance
Would be his nations secret grievance
He would die for his disobedience

Heartbreaker
She swings in a smile on her face
Wearing high heels satin and lace
But beware of her and her fast pace
Cause she's a heartbreaker fallen from grace

A heartbreaker in experience born
She was cast down and her wings were shorn
Flung down by just such a fake-
Now she's a heartbreaker fallen from grace

She's loud and she's boisterous and plenty of fun
But she now is out to do what's been done
Many have tried to save that pretty face
But she's a heartbreaker fallen from grace.

The deep set eyes and perilous gaze
Entrapping hearts like a starlet on stage
She once loved but has lost her place
Oh what a travesty fallen from grace

February 14
February 14
Dawns bright and fair
Yet Something is up
An ominous air

Girls are pumped
I haven't a clue
What have I missed
What's the to do?

As a guy I feel a brooding
like some coming storm
Yet the weather is fine
The day seems the norm

Busted
Hand in the cookie jar-
The lights come on.
A face of innocence,
And a sticky paw.
Busted

Protesting your honesty-
But caught on a tape.
Someone was sneaky,
And wired the place.
Busted

To walk in integrity-
It is hard to do
But to live in the dark,
Is to play peakaboo.
Busted

Scars
I've been places that I regret
I've seen things I can-not forget
I've done stuff I can't undo
So I want to help –help you

These scars that you see
And the ones underneath
I want to save you-
Walk in Christ's peace

The tears of anguish
The pains that distinguish
Are better never attained
He's paid the way

What do You do when God is calling
What do You do when God is calling
What do you do when you hear your name
What do you do in his awesome presence
Do you sow leaves or hide in shame

The young boy Samuel was lying in his bed
hearing strange voices and bumping his head
Then at last he knew the truth
God was working in the life of this youth

What do You do when God is calling
What do you do when you hear your name
If God says go will you obey in fullness
Or will you fall into Balaam's shame

David was standing watching the sheep
When he was sent for by Samuel the seer
He did not hide or run away
A man after God's heart he said okay

What do You do when God is calling
What will you do when Jesus says hey
If God says go will you obey in fullness
Or will you fall into darkest shame

Made in United States
Orlando, FL
23 February 2022